T0065177

MANNA:
THE LORD'S SUPPER

IT'S THE PARTY OF THE MILLENNIUM Y'ALL! YOU'RE INVITED!

Volume 35

Jesus Christ Superstar! Studio 3 Selection For Men. Outback 5 Blade. THE PRISONERS ARE SET FREE TODAY.

John F. Kennedy #35- The "bad thief" on the Cross! [G.O.A.T]

He Comes Suddenly to His Temple and the Day Burns as an Oven in McCartyhy's Bakersville Home in California.

QUEEN OLYMPIA VICTORIA

authorHOUSE

AuthorHouse™
1663 Liberty Drive
Bloomington, IN 47403
www.authorhouse.com
Phone: 833-262-8899

Published by AuthorHouse 01/13/2023

ISBN: 978-1-7283-7757-5 (sc)
ISBN: 978-1-7283-7756-8 (e)

CONTENTS

INTRODUCTION

Today is Sabbath January 7, 2023 and the time is ripe. (7:07 am)

Yesterday on January 6, 2023 I sounded The Loud Cry of Revelation 18, when I sent off the manuscript for the 5th Book with 13 volumes to Author House Publishing for publication. These messages are pertinent at this time because they announce the fall of Babylon and how to escape the burning in the aftermath of her destruction! The Word of God is indeed sharper than a two-edged sword. "For the word of God is quick, and powerful, and sharper than any two edged sword, piercing even to the dividing asunder of soul and spirit, and of the joints and marrow, and is a discerner of the thoughts and intents of the heart."

Hebrew 4:12

CHAPTER ONE

When Nancy Pelosi's husband Paul Pelosi was attacked by a Hammer wielding assailant at his home in November 2022 it was a sign of the hammer of God breaking the nations and hammering them out at this time. The hammer eventually landed in the GOP controlled House and talked with the Speaker to be Kevin McCarthy. God told him that He was about to establish His kingdom of righteousness in Palestine and he needed to get the code for this kingdom from Donald Trump in Mar-a -Lago. Time:7:27 am

Donald Trump had already announced the Eleventh Hour workers in a code he gave to Raffensperger when he was searching for extra votes after the 2020 election.

The ever dutiful Speaker whom the Mogul calls "My Kevin" went to collect the code after the January 6 insurrection of the Capitol (2022)and secured it for the following year.(2023)

Havoc in the House- McCarthy wins Speaker after a wild vote.

"It took **14** failed votes and days of being publicly humiliated, but hey, the California Republican got what he wanted."

The Republican's Rocky path to leadership was by God's design to call forth the hour of judgment on the earth. **Kevin Owen McCarthy** whose initials number **39** is a symbol of the kingdom. His middle initial **O** has taken us full circle to the **vanishing hour, Omicron,** and the **Ides of March.** Kevin's middle initial **O** is different from Alexandria **Ocasio's "O"** which means Omega.

K.   O.   M.

Kingd   O   M
Matthew Chapter 6.

Thy kingdom come. Thy will be done on earth as it is in heaven.

So while Kevin McCarthy made **15 turns** on the Dial of Ahaz (Isaiah) to bring an end to sin and usher in everlasting righteousness and peace, his wife Judy Wages highlights the plight of those who owe debts at the end of their tenure and must pay the price with their own blood. Judy Wages is now making the announcement with her name that Christ has come back to reward every man according to his work." And, behold, I come quickly; and my reward is with me, to give every man according as his work shall be." REvelation 22:12

Sir Popeye was given a Tesla and the name meaning is "of the ax" and "harvester".

Those who are faithful and have the seal of God will inherit the kingdom forever more. Those who are unfaithful like the first thief on the cross who despised his salvation will burn at last in an oven prepared for the lost. (Malachi 3.)The number 35th President **JFK** represented a class of abandoned sinners who glorify the basest parts of human nature. The curse of sin never glorifies but always ends in disgrace. Why was 24 year old Bills Safety Damar Hamlin spared and not 24 year old Dwayne Haskins of the Pittsburgh Steelers? One had the seal of the living God and the other did not.

Jesus Christ has returned in His invisible form in the person of His living saints -the 144,000 servants of the Most High. He comes in to disclose them to view as emergency workers to save the world now in crisis and on the brink of collapse. The **OUTBACK 5 BLADE** is the five book series of Manna that is equivalent to David's five smooth stones that were used to sever the giant's head. With the Word of God we will slay the enemy and recover the kingdom.

THE ROARING OF THE BEAST. GET READY! GET READY! GET READY!

When the enemy sees that he has lost out, he will get enraged and turn on the followers of the purified church to persecute them. (Revelation13)The Mark of the Beast system will make an image of the beast replicating the dark ages of Roman apostasy. Those who accept the image beast will be consumed while those who reject its sophostries will be spared. Notice that Kevin McCarthy is from Bakersfield and his father was a firechief. The fire of God is in the land. Beware! So then, when my friend Jo-Ann Richards-Goffe says **"KOM MEK WI WORSHIP"** to which God will you bow down in Jimmy Carter's Plain of Dura? The true and living God of heaven and earth or to the gods of Baal? President Carter, a true worshiper of the Most High, is the 39th president of the United States who lives in Plains, Georgia witnessing to a generation that we are on the verge of entering the Promised land as our days of wilderness wanderings are over!

THE CHURCH HAS SUFFERED VIOLENCE. WE TAKE THE KINGDOM BY FORCE!

The children of darkness hate the children of light why Prince William of Britain attacked Prince Harry over his choice of a wife-Meghan Markle. The Prince of Sussex, Harry represents the guests at the Marriage supper in the age of the Great Consummation. He has since discarded his filthy "Nazi" garments and chosen the pure white robe of Christ's righteousness offered to all marriage guests. Christ rewarded him with a first born son Archie who would represent the last Adam to the human race. We got our dominion back with the birth of Master Archie! We have all been **spared** from sin's ruin and disaster. We have been redeemed by His blood and are saved.

We Enter Into Our Glorious Rest On Sabbath January 7,2023. Time:10:08 am

"The thief cometh not, but for to steal, and to kill, and to destroy: I am come that they might have life, and that they might have it more abundantly." John 10:10

Christ will never take anything from us that is for our good. All He asks is that we give Him our sins in exchange for His righteousness. He offers us a robe white as snow in exchange for our filthy garments. Make the exchange today. Christ by His death on the cross has given us a new lease on life. We do not have to live on the lowlands of sin and misery anymore.

"But as it is written, Eye hath not seen, nor ear heard, neither have entered into the heart of man, the things which God hath prepared for them that love him." 1 Corinthians 2:9

Brethren, it will be joy unspeakable and full of glory.1 Peter 1:8

Letting go of the darkness in 2022.

Error is a parasite that lives on the tree of truth. The manifestation of darkness is the full number **92** and when reversed by light it becomes **29.**The very first component of darkness is **41** which is a backway kingdom(**14**).The manifestation of light is the pure word from **A-Z** numbering **26** on the English alphabet. When the first component of darkness (41) at 4182 Indian Manor Stone Mountain is added to the light (26) in the 26 cents in the Red purse in Ohio, we get **67** years of Emmett Till. Thus we shout "Awake My Soul and Sing" for the night is past. The light of present truth has overtaken the darkness at last! We, like Emmett Till, are made into Movie Stars because we are the seed of Abraham, our father. We will shine as stars in the firmament of our God and King.**67 years and it's the end of our long and trying journey.67 years and the longest road must end! Amen.**

Speaker Anunciata Pelosi during the harvest period and McCarthy's "fifteen minutes of fame." Time 3:31 am Sunday morning January 8.

Speaker Pelosi's tenure as Speaker of the House of Representatives was symbolic of the harvest period in which members of the church had the opportunity to get the seal of God and be saved. When her tenure was up, it meant the end of the harvest and the start of the judgment in the house of God. (1 Peter 4:17)

McCarthy's tenure then will begin the period of reaping when probation is closed for the church and there is time no longer. The 15 rounds of voting for the Speaker that took 4 -days represent the entire span of human redemption. There are four divisions of time that will herald the end and bring about a revival and reformation in the land.

1. **15x 100= 1500**
2. **15x 100= 1500**
3. **15x 100=1500**
4. **15x 100=1500**

A grand total of 6000 years. The End of time.

1500x4= 6000 years.

Martin Luther started the reformation in **1500 AD** and that reformation dealt a blow to the Papacy creating a "deadly wound."

The **430** years of bondage that the children of Israel suffered ended in **1930 (1500+ 430)** when the message of the Shepherd's Rod came with Present Truth and meat in due season. We are the repairers of the breach and God's battle axe and weapons of war. So with Nancy gone there is no hope for the Laodiceans or the Esauites in the church as there is found no place for repentance when the Bakersville man takes the gavel from Pelosi's hand. (Nancy! Where are you Nancy?) The fifteen minutes of grace has run out on the church and now it's **Doomsday** for them. **Doomsday!** (3:53 am)

Meanwhile in the camp of the sealed one is rejoicing and happiness beyond measure.

- We are the Bees knees while the rest are potato heads. Tags: **53831 Black car.**

Silver Explorer CTE 6085. Darkness **vacates the scene! Let the marriage supper begin.1985.**

So while there was a chance for the church to get the seal during the speakership of Pelosi, the chance no longer exists under McCarthy who brings an end to sin's reign in the church and usher in righteousness and peace at last. The 144,00 saints are sealed before the slaughter of Ezekiel 9.

The Deputy Speaker of the House, Hakeem Jeffries in his **alphabet speech** gave birth to the light of the ZLoud Cry message thereby ushering in truth and righteousness and slamming shut the gates of hell. The **alphabet speech** numbering **26,** is the counterpart to the **26 cents** found in the red purse in Ohio that represents the light. The message eradicated the rogue Republicans who represent the darkness of evil in the number **41.(26+41=67)**

So, Hakeem really represents the kinetic energy (K E) that was once our covering in the Garden of Eden that is now restored to us!

This "ackee" also symbolizes the keys to the kingdom of glory. **Hello Ketanji!** The pocket monster has been captured at last-Trump the mystery of iniquity number two and Andrew Jackson, the mystery of iniquity number one. (the anti christs).Hurray, Hurray, Hurray!

Amen.

CHAPTER TWO

A REFRESHING DREAM

———

Norbert was driving a bus filled with Belvedere church members when he had to maneuver near a precipice on a steep hill. He had to muster all his strength to navigate the treacherous terrain. Members aboard the bus included Elder Mclain, Elder Carter and Dr. Consuela Bennett. At one point they all got out and began walking past houses along the way. The Senior Pastor Bulgin remarked that "Judith, the Davidian is with the group and her hair is in plaits!" My hair was plaited in two braids and joined at the bottom of my nape. The dream then changed to something else.

This dream represents the people of God walking about after the winter of sin is past and Spring comes along. The Spring of hope is here as was evidenced by the tenure of former speaker of the House, Paul Ryan of Wisconsin. The **114**th Congress confirmed Ryan as the **54**th Speaker of the United States House of Representatives on October 29,2015. Wisconsin was admitted to the Union on May

29,1848.Kevin O.McCarthy was waiting in the wings to be elected as Speaker, but a scandal caused him to withdraw. Ryan supported Donald Trump in his run for president of the United states in the 2016 elections.

Since Ryan is from Wisconsin, America's Dairyland it meant the saints had arrived in a land flowing with milk and honey. Wisconsin therefore highlights the fact that **Wisdom Conquers Sin** anyday, anytime, anywhere! **WISDOM CONQUERS SIN.** The machinery to destroy the saints could not be implemented before the material for the Loud Cry was ready. O the wisdom of my God!

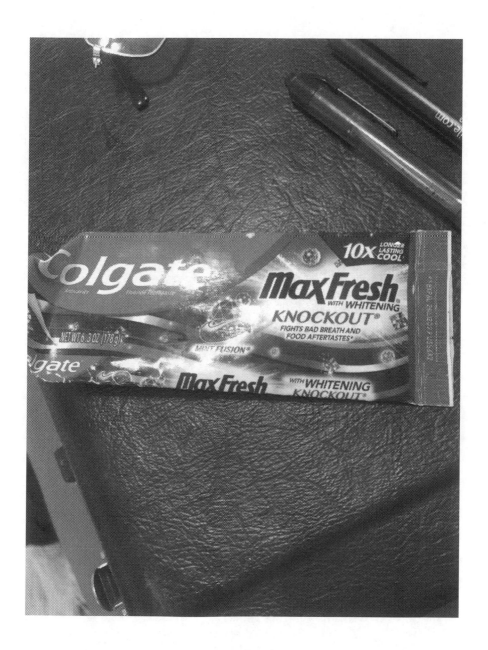

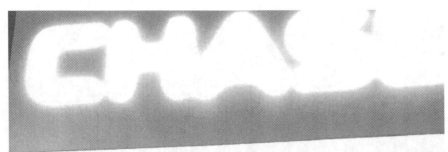

Choose your bills:
$5 $20 $100

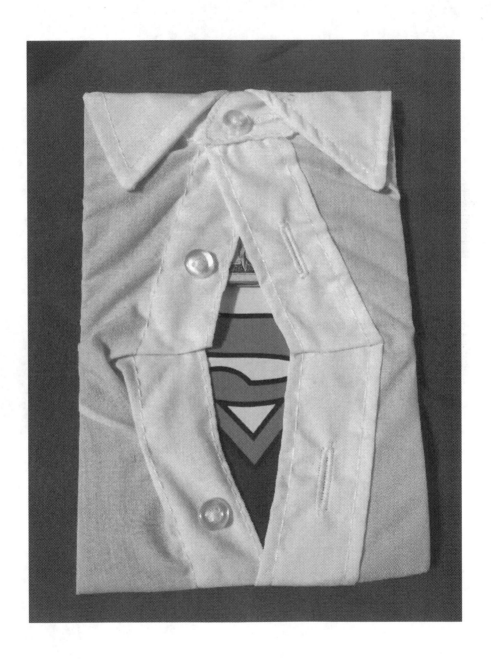

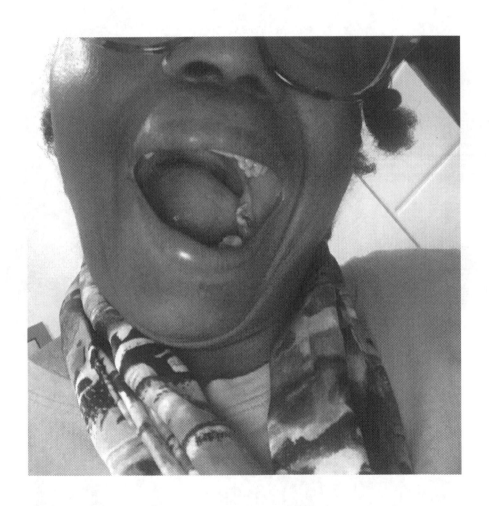

CHAPTER THREE

MY RAPUNZEL PLAITS

My plaited hair in the dream reflects the glory of the written Word as it lightens the earth with its glory. This takes us to Nebraska and the Platte River with its many tributaries.

The quaint Platte River State Park is nestled halfway between Nebraska's two largest cities-Lincoln and Omaha.

We remember Lincoln for his Gettysburg address and the "new birth of freedom" and Omaha for the wish granted to all who "ask" in faith believing they will receive from Mother earth and smile!

Before it was a state park it was two separate camps-Harriet Harding Campfire Girls Camp-(Five Foolish Virgins) and Camp Esther K.Newman-(Five Wise Virgins who shine as stars) and a tract of woodland. The charming vintage cabins that once housed campers today provide cozy accommodations while the gorgeous new glamping cabins offer a luxurious yet nature-immersive experience.

Contact Information
Address:Platte River State Park
| 14421 346th St| Louisville,
NE 68037-3001
Phone:(402)234-2217

So you see, we finally made it home having separated ourselves from the unbelieving ones. The 144,000 living saints were introduced in 2021.The first light bill that I got from Georgia Power was for $144.21.Please pay by Nov.16,2021.

The glory of the Lord shall be revealed and all flesh shall see it together. All iniquity workers will be cut off and the unclean ones barred from entrance in St. Louis. The last four-digits of phone number **(404)234-2217)** indicates the final separation in the church as the so-called believers telephone God for help! **2217** details 22 as the year 2022 and the final straw, and 17 as the last seventeen years for the church starting in Louisville Missouri in 2005 at the General Conference and ending in 2022 at the same place and time and the same General Conference. The Laodiceans lost were not transformed by grace. They did not grow and develop according to plan.

Now that the season of growing is over, they must be cut down as cumberers to the ground. The Coffee Bean grout stone in a blue plastic shield representing evil was placed in the red Status **Edge** bag yesterday to indicate the unclean ones entering their **inglorious rest.**

Oh, how glad are we who accepted up-to-date truth so we can live thereby! How glad we are that we embraced this miracle working truth that saves and sets the **prisoner free. We in our ackee with Minority House Representative hAKEEm.**

Satan's prison house is now empty as the prisoners' chains are gone and they are walking free! Herein lies the naked truth and I am not ashamed. No, I am not ashamed! We will soon become household names. Lol. Amen. Time:11:44 am.

Hallelujah to the Lamb of God.

Monday January 9,2023 Time: 6:45 am

Last night I purchased a black KING SIZE comforter set for Bunty and Laura's wedding gift on Amazon.

$74.71

CHAPTER FOUR

DREAMS

———◦◦◦◦———

In the dream I had, I was at a house cleaning up the kitchen are when a fire broke out in the plumbing area by the pipes. I got alarmed and used a piece of clothing to dampen the area and put out the fire. It went out but later reignited at another section of the pipes and I had to put it out by smothering it with a pillow. Then my sister Dacia, now deceased joined me and saw the fire again and told me to call 9-11. I told her if it gets too out of control and starts to blaze I would. Luckily it was put out this last time when I smothered it. Afterwards I went into the dining room and on the table were fresh green bundles of callaloo, cherry bush and other greens like the cocoa plant ready to be used up. The bundles were short and thick and of a living green color. End.

The black comforter for $74.71 is a symbol of the darkness to envelope the 5-foolish virgins who have run out of extra oil and have nothing in their vessels to guide them to the end of their journey. These five foolish virgins are the thirsty ones who never had the hunger for righteousness! Matthew 5.

"That everyone who **thirsteth** for the truth may obtain it, this booklet of questions and answers is, as a Christian service, mailed without charge. Send for it. It levies but one exaction, the souls obligation to itself to prove all things and hold fast that which is good. The only strings attached to this free proffer are the **golden strands of Eden and the crimson cords of Calvary- the ties that bind.**

Names and addresses of Seventh -Day adventists will be appreciated.

The Answerer
Book No.4

Questions and answers on Present Truth Topics in the interest of the Seventh -Day Adventist Brethren and Readers of

The Shepherd's Rod
By V.T Houteff

This "scribe" instructed unto the kingdom of heaven, "bringeth forth...things new and old." Matthew 13:52

Now sanctify the Lord God in your hearts :and be ready always to give an **answer** to every man that asketh you a reason of the hope that is in you with meekness and fear. <u>**1 Peter 3:15**</u>

CHAPTER FIVE

THE ANSWERER BOOK NO. 4

God is moved out of His holy habitation to punish all evil doers. The treatment given to NFL Safety Damar Hamlin by Roger "Farmer in the Dell" Goodell is exemplary. When he collapsed on the field he was resuscitated and taken to hospital and everyone prayed. When he recovered Goodell ordered the NFL teams to wear #3 t-Shirts in honor of Damar and his recovery. What a noble gesture! Damar on his part asked for continued prayers! Now this is how God wants His Children, especially His black boys-seed of Abraham to be treated by white folks. Satan wanted to wipe out the seed of Lo-ami by using the Police Federation to exterminate the blacks, but God has taken away the "Lo" and calls Ami "My people". Hosea 1&2

Yesterday they threw Emmett Till in the Mississippi River and today he is on the silver screen.

The Time To Make Great Headway is Now!

In the year 1930, God again spoke to His people, as He spoke to Israel in the days of Joshua, but now, as then, there are among us the ten spies, the Korahs, Dathans, and Abirams, and the Achans- all such as love to make discouraging reports, who seek position, who covet the Babylonish garment, the silver, and the wedge of gold. And as a result, we also are held back, and continue to be until the Lord manifests His power and takes from among us the pretending ones, makes us free from sin and sinners, as in the time of Korah and as in the time of Achan, and says to us as He said to Joshua, **"Go over this Jordan, thou, and all this people, unto the land which I do give to them, even to the children of Israel." Joshua 1:2**

Our Commander is leading out and we are victorious! The numbers we use help us understand whether we are coming or going or at a standstill. They light up our pathway to the kingdom. The world will soon be at our doorstep. Amen. The 40- year Wilderness experience is over. Now show me how you feel since you came outta wilderness! Bunty's wedding is the reception for all the wanderers who made it home. Luke 15.

Amen.

Tuesday January 10, 2023. Time: 5:00 am

From Thralldom to the Kingdom
Behold the Bridegroom cometh Go ye out to meet Him.
Matthew 25

The words, Arise, contend thou before the mountains, and let the hills hear thy voice, imply that heretofore his voice has been heard

Printed in the United States
by Baker & Taylor Publisher Services